AUDIO ACCESS INCLUDED

IMPROVISATION FOR CELLO OR BASS
MADE EASY

BY LAURIE GABRIEL

T0077052

ISBN 978-1-4950-9656-3

PLAYBACK+
Speed • Pitch • Balance • Loop

To access audio visit:
www.halleonard.com/mylibrary

Enter Code
5184-4184-1511-7538

Accompaniment Arrangements by Laurie Gabriel
Audio Production by Peter Deneff

7777 W. Bluemound Rd. P.O. Box 13819 Milwaukee, WI 53213

In Australia Contact:
Hal Leonard Australia Pty. Ltd.
4 Lentara Court
Cheltenham, Victoria, 3192 Australia
Email: ausadmin@halleonard.com.au

Visit Hal Leonard Online at
www.halleonard.com

HOW TO USE
IMPROVISATION FOR CELLO OR BASS MADE EASY

IT'S EASY!

The first group plays vamp one and repeats. Add in a second group on vamp two. Add in a third group on vamp three. Then add a soloist with his/her own improvisational creation! Use this format with several different soloists to perform the pieces in a concert setting! When soloists are finished, take out one vamp at a time until you're back to just the first vamp—or come up with your own big finish! Pieces can be played with or without the accompaniment tracks.

WORKS FOR ALL LEVELS!

A note to teachers: some of the rhythms may seem too advanced for your students; however, they can be quickly picked up by rote imitation until students become accustomed to the written rhythms. If any of the vamp lines are too difficult, choose the easiest vamp and use it alone. If you have mixed ability levels, give the harder vamps to your more advanced students. You can also leave out the vamps entirely and have your students improvise with the accompaniment. Try slowing down the accompaniment tracks using the *PLAYBACK+* software, or leave the accompaniment out entirely.

LOTS OF VARIATIONS!

Change the vamps, tempos, or solos to make each piece your own. The suggested activities on each page can be interchanged among all the pieces. Add your own ideas! Create other vamps using percussion instruments! There are lots of things to try. Composition can also be reinforced by writing solos down.

TIPS FOR SOLOISTS

1. Relax! It's impossible to evaluate yourself while simultaneously creating a solo. Leave all your judgements behind and let go. There are no mistakes; this is your creation.

2. Try keeping your solo within the "groove" of the background vamps. When first starting, choose a repeating rhythm and play it on just one note. Then, keep the same rhythm but change the notes up a bit. Gradually bring in more rhythmic variations and more notes.

3. Don't forget the wide variety of sounds that are available to you on a stringed instrument: pizzicato, tremolo, slides, trills, various bow styles from staccato to legato, percussive sounds against the body of the instrument, chop (striking the strings percussively with the bow), harmonics, double stops, ricochet bowing, accents, and anything else you can think of!

4. Listen to the mood of the piece. What emotions do you want to bring out in your playing?

5. Remember that silence (rests) can also be part of a solo.

6. When using the suggested notes for soloing, pay attention to which notes sound better as shorter "passing tones." This will become easier as you practice.

7. Keep trying. The more you improvise, the easier it gets!

1. Samurai

Part 1

Part 2

Part 3

Suggested notes for soloing: B, C♯, D, E, F♯, G, A

Try this: teacher plays a two-bar example; students echo as a group.

Concepts reinforced: B minor scale, 4/4 time, eighth rest, slur, double up-bow, parallel fourths

2. Hip Dawg

Suggested notes for soloing: A, B, C, D, E, F, G

Try this: teacher plays a different two-bar example for each
individual student to echo.

Concepts reinforced: A minor scale, 4/4 time, sixteenth notes, eighth rest, pizzicato

3. I Spy

Suggested notes for soloing: E, F#, G, A, B, C, D

Try this: student plays a two-bar example for the class to echo as a group.

Concepts reinforced: E minor scale, 4/4 time, tremolo, accent, arco/pizzicato transition

4. Solid Rock

Part 1

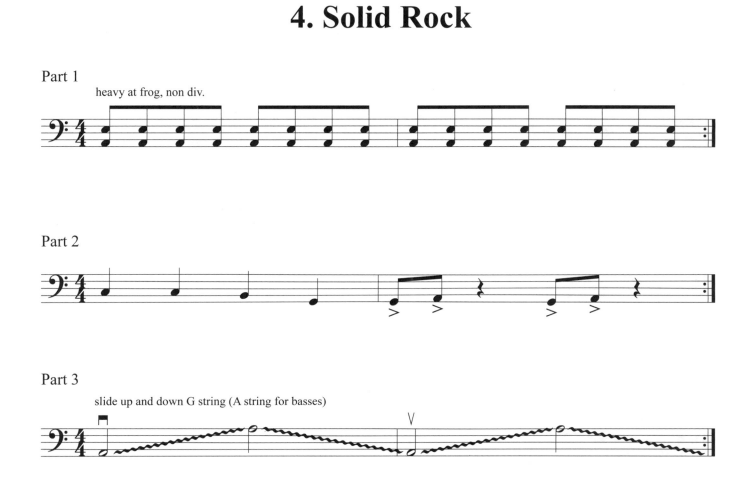

Suggested notes for soloing: A, B, C, D, E, F, G

Try this: student plays a different two-bar example for each student to echo.

Concepts reinforced: A minor scale, 4/4 time, double stop, accent, sliding

5. Hypnosis

Suggested notes for soloing: D, E, F, G, A, B♭, C

Try this: two or more soloists take turns playing two-bar improvisations (trading twos).

Concepts reinforced: D minor scale, 4/4 time, half position, octave jumps, sliding

6. Walk the Plank

Part 1

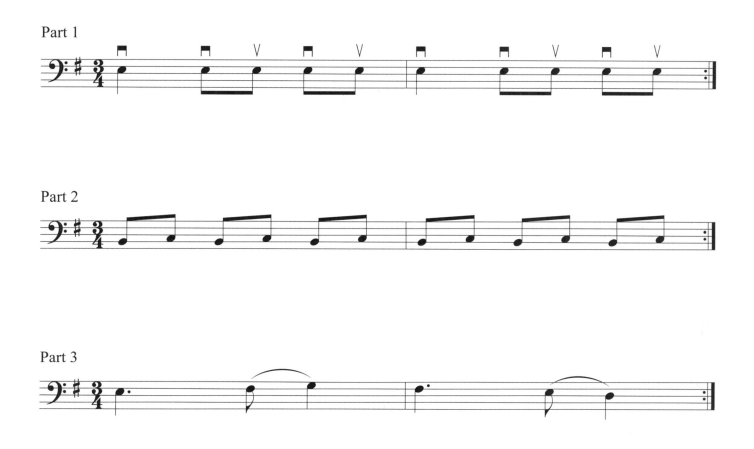

Part 2

Part 3

Suggested notes for soloing: E, F♯, G, A, B, C, D

Try this: two or more soloists take turns playing four-bar improvisations (trading fours).

Concepts reinforced: E minor scale, 3/4 time, double down-bow, dotted quarter note, slur

7. Snow Bells

Suggested notes for soloing: G, A, B, C, D, E, F♯

Try this: two or more soloists take turns playing eight-bar improvisations (trading eights).

Concepts reinforced: G major scale, 4/4 time, sixteenth notes, accent, slur, pizzicato

8. Oktoberfest

Part 1

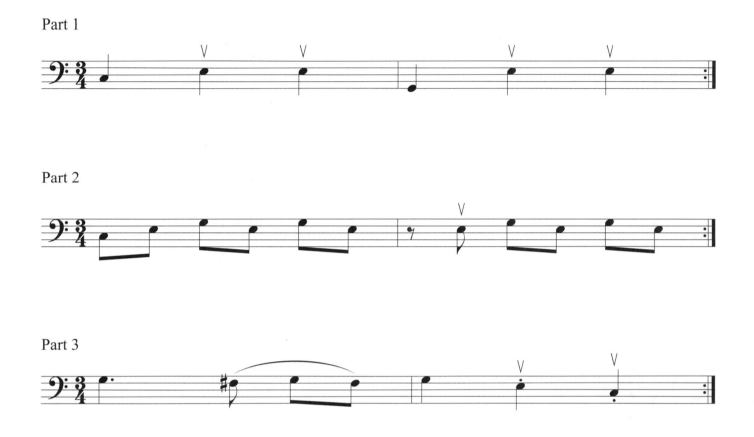

Part 2

Part 3

Suggested notes for soloing: C, D, E, F, G, A, B

Try this: entire class tries soloing at once with the background track.

Concepts reinforced: C major scale, 3/4 time, dotted quarter note, double up-bow, slur, staccato

9. Music Box

Part 1

Part 2

Part 3

Suggested notes for soloing: D, E, F♯, G, A, B, C♯

Try this: work in quartets with only one person on each vamp and one soloist.
Then rotate parts.

Concepts reinforced: D major scale, 3/4 time, eighth rest, double stop pizzicato

10. Space Bubbles

Part 1

Suggested notes for soloing: A, B, C, D, E, F, G

Try this: create a solo that uses only one note but different rhythms.

Concepts reinforced: A minor scale, 4/4 time, octave jumps, double down-bows, pizzicato

11. Land Ahoy

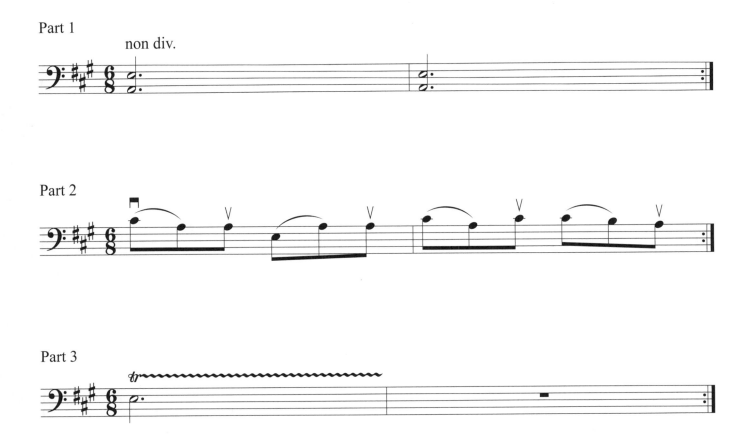

Suggested notes for soloing: A, B, C♯, D, E, F♯, G♯

Try this: sing a solo using nonsense syllables, rhymes, or even silly sentences.

Concepts reinforced: A major scale, 6/8 time, double stop, slur, trill

12. Cathedral Chant

Part 1

Part 2

Part 3

Suggested notes for soloing: E, F♯, G, A, B, C, D

Try this: sing and play a solo simultaneously.

Concepts reinforced: E minor scale, 4/4 time, double stop, pizzicato

13. Lasso Loop

Part 1

Part 2

Part 3

Suggested notes for soloing: G, A, B, C, D, E, F♯

Try this: soloist sings a two-bar improvisation for others to echo,
or plays it back himself/herself.

Concepts reinforced: G major scale, 12/8 time, slur, tie, pizzicato, long bows

14. Taj Mahal

Part 1

Part 2

Part 3

Suggested notes for soloing: C, D, E, F, G, A, B

Try this: soloist plays or sings a four-bar improvisation for others to echo.

Concepts reinforced: C major scale, 4/4 time, dotted quarter notes, sixteenth notes, offbeat, slur

15. Kyoto Rain

Part 1

Part 2

Part 3

Part 4 (*optional*)
Pat hands rapidly on legs for rain sound effect.

Suggested notes for soloing: G, A, B, D, E

Try this: soloist plays or sings an eight-bar improvisation for others to echo.

Concepts reinforced: pentatonic scale, 4/4 time, sixteenth notes, staccato, slur

16. Desert Dunes

Part 1

Part 2

Part 3

Suggested notes for soloing: G, A, B♭, C, D, E♭, F

Try this: write a solo down. Of course, then it's not quite improvisation anymore–but it's good practice for composition!

Concepts reinforced: G minor scale, 4/4 time, dotted half note, slur

17. Bottle Bounce

Part 1

(arco)

Part 2

(arco)

Part 3

pizz.

Part Four (*optional*)
Blow into bottles or tap on water glasses of various sizes.

Suggested notes for soloing: B♭, C, D, E♭, F, G, A

Try this: play a solo that includes whistling.

Concepts reinforced: B♭ major scale, 4/4 time, offbeat, slur, louré bowing

18. Fiddlin' Fool

Part 1

Part 2

Part 3

Suggested notes for soloing: D, E, F♯, G, A, B, C♯

Try this: find as many well-known songs as you can
(Mary Had a Little Lamb, Hot Cross Buns, etc.) that fit with the vamp.

Concepts reinforced: D major scale, 4/4 time, sliding, double stop, grace notes, double down-bow

19. Pastorale

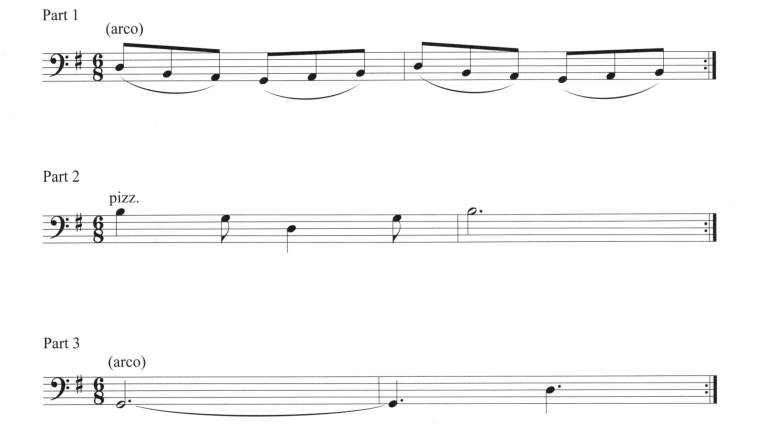

Suggested notes for soloing: G, A, B, C, D, E, F♯

Try this: make up a fourth vamp.

Concepts reinforced: G major scale, 6/8 time, triplets, tie, slur, pizzicato, long bows

20. Surfer Dude

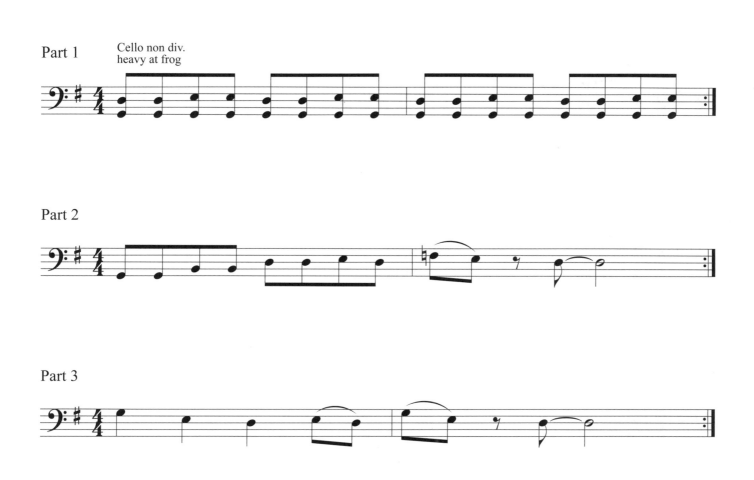

Suggested notes for soloing: G, A, B, C, D, E, F♮

Try this: make up a fourth vamp using only body percussion.

Concepts reinforced: G major scale, 4/4 time, tie, syncopation, double stop, slur, minor seventh

21. Disco Ball

Part 1

Part 2

Part 3

Suggested notes for soloing: G, A, B♭, C, D, E♭, F

Try this: play your vamp in a different octave than written.

Concepts reinforced: G minor scale, 4/4 time, sixteenth notes, octave jumps, slur

22. Highland Moors

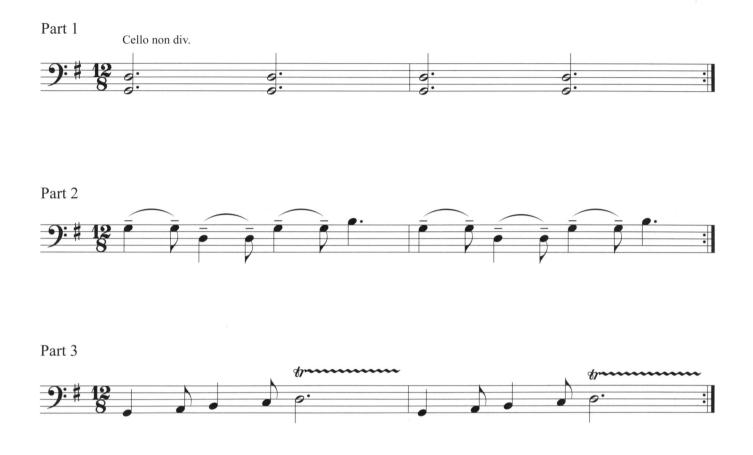

Part 1

Cello non div.

Part 2

Part 3

Suggested notes for soloing: G, A, B, C, D, E, F♯

Try this: each time you repeat your vamp, alternate between loud and soft.

Concepts reinforced: G major scale, 12/8 time, hooked bowing, trill, double stop

23. Broken String Blues

Part 1

Part 2

Part 3

Suggested notes for soloing: G, A, B, C, D, E, F♮

Try this: play a solo that alternates between two bars of soft and two bars of loud.

Concepts reinforced: 4/4 time, triplet swing feel, tie, double stop, minor seventh, walking bass line

24. Island Groove

Part 1

Part 2

Part 3

Suggested notes for soloing: E, F♯, G, A, B, C, D

Try this: play a solo that includes harmonics.

Concepts reinforced: E minor scale, 4/4 time, tie, dotted eighth, sixteenth note, tremolo, pizzicato

25. Powdered Wig

Part 1

Part 2

pizz.

Part 3

(arco)

Suggested notes for soloing: G, A, B, C, D, E, F♯

Try this: play a solo that includes trills.

Concepts reinforced: G major scale, 4/4 time, dotted eighth note, staccato, pizzicato

26. Tribal Ancestors

Part 1

Part 2

Part 3

Suggested notes for soloing: F♯, G♯, A, B, C♯, D, E

Try this: keeping the rhythms the same, find different notes that work for each vamp.

Concepts reinforced: F♯ minor scale, 4/4 time, dotted half note, double up-bow, staccato, accent

27. Shoreline

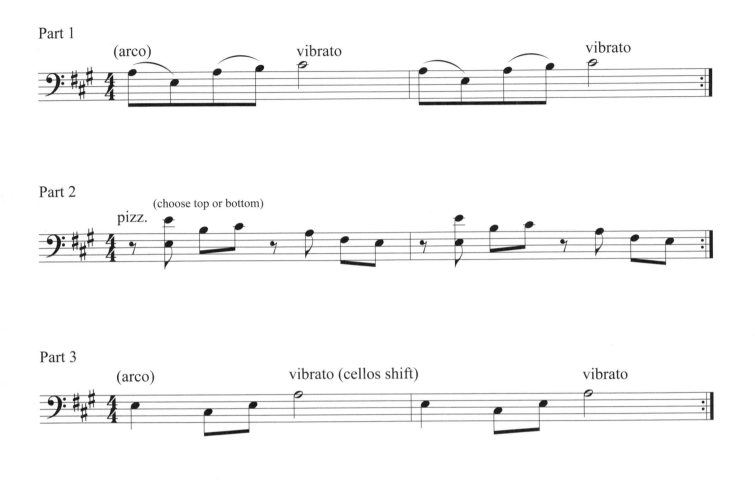

Suggested notes for soloing: A, B, C♯, D, E, F♯, G♯

Try this: play a solo all on one string, shifting for higher notes.

Concepts reinforced: A major scale, 4/4 time, offbeat, slur, legato, vibrato

28. Southern Revival

Part 1

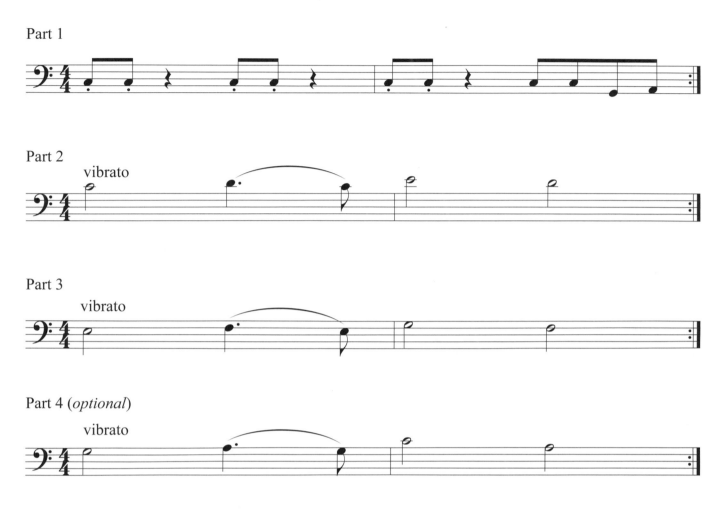

Part 2

vibrato

Part 3

vibrato

Part 4 (*optional*)

vibrato

Suggested notes for soloing: C, D, E, F, G, A, B

Try this: vamps two, three, and four sing your part on the syllable "Oh".
You could also sing and play simultaneously, or sing one part and play another!

Concepts reinforced: C major scale, 4/4 time, dotted quarter note, slur, staccato, legato

29. Headstones

Part 1

Part 2

Part 3

Suggested notes for soloing: G, A, B♭, C, D, E♭, F

Try this: play a solo that alternates between two bars of staccato and two bars of legato.

Concepts reinforced: G minor scale, 4/4 time, sixteenth notes, sixteenth rests, accent, slur

30. String Swing

Part 1

pizz.

Part 2

(arco)

Part 3

(arco)

Suggested notes for soloing: F, G, A, B♭, C, D, E

Try this: soloist plays an eight-bar improvisation, then points to
another student who must take over soloing. Continue until all have played a solo.

Concepts reinforced: F major scale, 4/4 time, triplet swing feel, tie, slur, walking bass line

31. Hot Sauce

Part 1

Part 2

Cello non div.

Part 3

Suggested notes for soloing: C, D, E, F, G, A, B

Try this: soloists and/or background players vocally make a "t-t-t-t-" sound
on the eighth note pulse (while simultaneously playing). It will sound like maracas!

Concepts reinforced: C major scale, 4/4 time, dotted quarter note, tie, syncopation, double stop

32. Klezmer

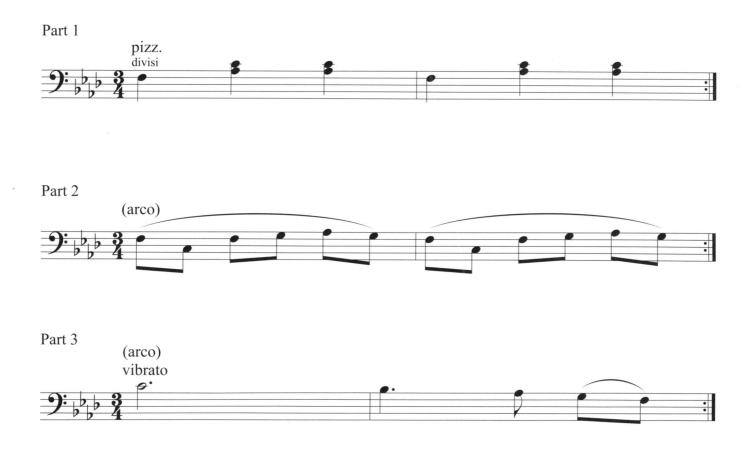

Part 1

Part 2

Part 3

Suggested notes for soloing: F, G, A♭, B♭, C, D♭, E♭

Try this: play solo that includes lots of sliding.

Concepts reinforced: F minor scale, 3/4 time, slur, legato, vibrato, divisi

33. Sand Storm

Part 1

Part 2

Part 3

Suggested notes for soloing: B♭, C, D♭, E♭, F, G♭, A♭

Try this: play a solo that includes some sort of percussive sound on your instrument (tapping the wood, hitting the bow against the strings, *col legno* bowing, etc.).

Concepts reinforced: B♭ minor scale, 4/4 time, sixteenth note, dotted quarter note, slur, pizzicato

34. Dub Kick

Part 1

Part 2

Part 3

Suggested notes for soloing: C, D, E♭, F, G, A♭, B♭

Try this: play a solo that is entirely tremolo.

Concepts reinforced: C minor scale, 4/4 time, sixteenth note, slur, legato

35. Game Over

Suggested notes for soloing: E♭, F, G, A♭, B♭, C, D

Try this: play a solo that is all quarter notes, all eighth notes, or all sixteenth notes.

Concepts reinforced: E♭ major scale, 4/4 time, syncopation, double up-bow, pizzicato, *louré* bowing

INDEX OF CONCEPTS REINFORCED

Your favorite songs are arranged just for solo instrumentalists with this outstanding series. Each book includes a great full-accompaniment play-along audio so you can sound just like a pro! Check out www.halleonard.com to see all the titles available.

The Beatles

All You Need Is Love • Blackbird • Day Tripper • Eleanor Rigby • Get Back • Here, There and Everywhere • Hey Jude • I Will • Let It Be • Lucy in the Sky with Diamonds • Ob-La-Di, Ob-La-Da • Penny Lane • Something • Ticket to Ride • Yesterday.

_____ 00225330	Flute	$14.99
_____ 00225331	Clarinet	$14.99
_____ 00225332	Alto Sax	$14.99
_____ 00225333	Tenor Sax	$14.99
_____ 00225334	Trumpet	$14.99
_____ 00225335	Horn	$14.99
_____ 00225336	Trombone	$14.99
_____ 00225337	Violin	$14.99
_____ 00225338	Viola	$14.99
_____ 00225339	Cello	$14.99

Chart Hits

All About That Bass • All of Me • Happy • Radioactive • Roar • Say Something • Shake It Off • A Sky Full of Stars • Someone like You • Stay with Me • Thinking Out Loud • Uptown Funk.

_____ 00146207	Flute	$12.99
_____ 00146208	Clarinet	$12.99
_____ 00146209	Alto Sax	$12.99
_____ 00146210	Tenor Sax	$12.99
_____ 00146211	Trumpet	$12.99
_____ 00146212	Horn	$12.99
_____ 00146213	Trombone	$12.99
_____ 00146214	Violin	$12.99
_____ 00146215	Viola	$12.99
_____ 00146216	Cello	$12.99

Coldplay

Clocks • Every Teardrop Is a Waterfall • Fix You • In My Place • Lost! • Paradise • The Scientist • Speed of Sound • Trouble • Violet Hill • Viva La Vida • Yellow.

_____ 00103337	Flute	$12.99
_____ 00103338	Clarinet	$12.99
_____ 00103339	Alto Sax	$12.99
_____ 00103340	Tenor Sax	$12.99
_____ 00103341	Trumpet	$12.99
_____ 00103342	Horn	$12.99
_____ 00103343	Trombone	$12.99
_____ 00103344	Violin	$12.99
_____ 00103345	Viola	$12.99
_____ 00103346	Cello	$12.99

Disney Greats

Arabian Nights • Hawaiian Roller Coaster Ride • It's a Small World • Look Through My Eyes • Yo Ho (A Pirate's Life for Me) • and more.

_____ 00841934	Flute	$12.99
_____ 00841935	Clarinet	$12.99
_____ 00841936	Alto Sax	$12.99
_____ 00841937	Tenor Sax	$12.95
_____ 00841938	Trumpet	$12.99
_____ 00841939	Horn	$12.99
_____ 00841940	Trombone	$12.95
_____ 00841941	Violin	$12.99
_____ 00841942	Viola	$12.99
_____ 00841943	Cello	$12.99
_____ 00842078	Oboe	$12.99

Great Themes

Bella's Lullaby • Chariots of Fire • Get Smart • Hawaii Five-O Theme • I Love Lucy • The Odd Couple • Spanish Flea • and more.

_____ 00842468	Flute	$12.99
_____ 00842469	Clarinet	$12.99
_____ 00842470	Alto Sax	$12.99
_____ 00842471	Tenor Sax	$12.99
_____ 00842472	Trumpet	$12.99
_____ 00842473	Horn	$12.99
_____ 00842474	Trombone	$12.99
_____ 00842475	Violin	$12.99
_____ 00842476	Viola	$12.99
_____ 00842477	Cello	$12.99

Popular Hits

Breakeven • Fireflies • Halo • Hey, Soul Sister • I Gotta Feeling • I'm Yours • Need You Now • Poker Face • Viva La Vida • You Belong with Me • and more.

_____ 00842511	Flute	$12.99
_____ 00842512	Clarinet	$12.99
_____ 00842513	Alto Sax	$12.99
_____ 00842514	Tenor Sax	$12.99
_____ 00842515	Trumpet	$12.99
_____ 00842516	Horn	$12.99
_____ 00842517	Trombone	$12.99
_____ 00842518	Violin	$12.99
_____ 00842519	Viola	$12.99
_____ 00842520	Cello	$12.99

Songs from Frozen, Tangled and Enchanted

Do You Want to Build a Snowman? • For the First Time in Forever • Happy Working Song • I See the Light • In Summer • Let It Go • Mother Knows Best • That's How You Know • True Love's First Kiss • When Will My Life Begin • and more.

_____ 00126921	Flute	$14.99
_____ 00126922	Clarinet	$14.99
_____ 00126923	Alto Sax	$14.99
_____ 00126924	Tenor Sax	$14.99
_____ 00126925	Trumpet	$14.99
_____ 00126926	Horn	$14.99
_____ 00126927	Trombone	$14.99
_____ 00126928	Violin	$14.99
_____ 00126929	Viola	$14.99
_____ 00126930	Cello	$14.99

Top Hits

Adventure of a Lifetime • Budapest • Die a Happy Man • Ex's & Oh's • Fight Song • Hello • Let It Go • Love Yourself • One Call Away • Pillowtalk • Stitches • Writing's on the Wall.

_____ 00171073	Flute	$12.99
_____ 00171074	Clarinet	$12.99
_____ 00171075	Alto Sax	$12.99
_____ 00171106	Tenor Sax	$12.99
_____ 00171107	Trumpet	$12.99
_____ 00171108	Horn	$12.99
_____ 00171109	Trombone	$12.99
_____ 00171110	Violin	$12.99
_____ 00171111	Viola	$12.99
_____ 00171112	Cello	$12.99

Wicked

As Long As You're Mine • Dancing Through Life • Defying Gravity • For Good • I'm Not That Girl • Popular • The Wizard and I • and more.

_____ 00842236	Flute	$12.99
_____ 00842237	Clarinet	$12.99
_____ 00842238	Alto Saxophone	$11.95
_____ 00842239	Tenor Saxophone	$11.95
_____ 00842240	Trumpet	$11.99
_____ 00842241	Horn	$11.95
_____ 00842242	Trombone	$12.99
_____ 00842243	Violin	$11.99
_____ 00842244	Viola	$12.99
_____ 00842245	Cello	$12.99

101 SONGS

YOUR FAVORITE SONGS ARE ARRANGED FOR SOLO INSTRUMENTALISTS WITH THIS GREAT SERIES.

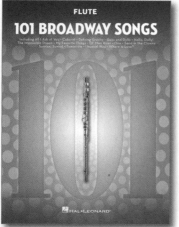

101 BROADWAY SONGS

Cabaret • Do You Hear the People Sing? • Edelweiss • Guys and Dolls • Hello, Dolly! • I Dreamed a Dream • If I Were a Bell • Luck Be a Lady • Ol' Man River • Seasons of Love • Send in the Clowns • Think of Me • Tomorrow • What I Did for Love • and many more.

00154199	Flute	$14.99
00154200	Clarinet	$14.99
00154201	Alto Sax	$14.99
00154202	Tenor Sax	$14.99
00154203	Trumpet	$14.99
00154204	Horn	$14.99
00154205	Trombone	$14.99
00154206	Violin	$14.99
00154207	Viola	$14.99
00154208	Cello	$14.99

101 HIT SONGS

All About That Bass • All of Me • Brave • Breakaway • Clocks • Fields of Gold • Firework • Hey, Soul Sister • Ho Hey • I Gotta Feeling • Jar of Hearts • Love Story • 100 Years • Roar • Rolling in the Deep • Shake It Off • Smells like Teen Spirit • Uptown Funk • and more.

00194561	Flute	$16.99
00197182	Clarinet	$16.99
00197183	Alto Sax	$16.99
00197184	Tenor Sax	$16.99
00197185	Trumpet	$16.99
00197186	Horn	$16.99
00197187	Trombone	$16.99
00197188	Violin	$16.99
00197189	Viola	$16.99
00197190	Cello	$16.99

101 CLASSICAL THEMES

Ave Maria • Bist du bei mir (You Are with Me) • Canon in D • Clair de Lune • Dance of the Sugar Plum Fairy • 1812 Overture • Eine Kleine Nachtmusik ("Serenade"), First Movement Excerpt • The Flight of the Bumble Bee • Funeral March of a Marionette • Fur Elise • Gymnopedie No. 1 • Jesu, Joy of Man's Desiring • Lullaby • Minuet in G • Ode to Joy • Piano Sonata in C • Pie Jesu • Rondeau • Theme from Swan Lake • Wedding March • William Tell Overture • and many more.

00155315	Flute	$14.99
00155317	Clarinet	$14.99
00155318	Alto Sax	$14.99
00155319	Tenor Sax	$14.99
00155320	Trumpet	$14.99
00155321	Horn	$14.99
00155322	Trombone	$14.99
00155323	Violin	$14.99
00155324	Viola	$14.99
00155325	Cello	$14.99

101 JAZZ SONGS

All of Me • Autumn Leaves • Bewitched • Blue Skies • Body and Soul • Cheek to Cheek • Come Rain or Come Shine • Don't Get Around Much Anymore • A Fine Romance • Here's to Life • I Could Write a Book • It Could Happen to You • The Lady Is a Tramp • Like Someone in Love • Lullaby of Birdland • The Nearness of You • On Green Dolphin Street • Satin Doll • Stella by Starlight • Tangerine • Unforgettable • The Way You Look Tonight • Yesterdays • and many more.

00146363	Flute	$14.99
00146364	Clarinet	$14.99
00146366	Alto Sax	$14.99
00146367	Tenor Sax	$14.99
00146368	Trumpet	$14.99
00146369	Horn	$14.99
00146370	Trombone	$14.99
00146371	Violin	$14.99
00146372	Viola	$14.99
00146373	Cello	$14.99

www.halleonard.com

Prices, contents and availability subject to change without notice.